On Wings of Grace

On Wings of Grace

Marilyn D. Donahue

Rev. date: 07/15/2020

To order additional copies of this book, contact:
Xlibris
1-888-795-4274
www.Xlibris.com
Orders@Xlibris.com
816705

Preface

"On Wings of Grace" is a compilation of poems and thoughts that acknowledge some of the events currently happening in this world, my reflections about them and my perspectives of our mortal existence in this life. Since the very moment of our first breath at birth, we have lived in this world, in this body; it is the only life we know. Throughout our years of growth and experiences, there are things we have learned about ourselves and the environment around us. Each new thought or encounter we go through, builds upon lessons already learned. Our perspectives or interactions in any situation are usually determined by our individual knowledge of and or by realities of this physical world we live in. Then, in those times when things happen that we just cannot explain; we need to pause, be still and take a look at life through spiritual eyes...to find Grace.

Grace is unmerited favor; it is not earned by merit or deeds. It is forgiveness, pardon and mercy, virtues given from God above. Grace is God's blessing to mankind, despite the sinfulness of our ways. Since those first days in the Garden of Eden, we have all come short of the Glory of God. With that said, it doesn't mean that God has given up on us; he gives us opportunities every day to seek his Word and strive to live a life that is pleasing in his sight. We may not always make the right decisions or do things we know we should do; but if we ask, God is faithful and just to forgive our sins. **Matthew 7:7 KJV, "Ask, and it shall be given you; seek, and ye shall find; knock and it shall be opened unto you:**

Every day that God allows us to live, is another day that we have to make a difference in this world or to make a difference in the lives of others. That difference doesn't always have to be something noted on a grand scale; it could be something as small as a kind word or gentle smile to someone who is going through a stressful time. It could also be as simple as helping someone to reach an item from a grocery store shelf. The thought is about selflessness, putting someone else's good before our own. There is an old adage of truth, "There is always someone worse off than you." God is aware of each of our needs and where we are in our lives; because he sees the bigger picture, he may sometimes allow people to cross our paths for those particular needs to be met.

We may not always understand or see the purpose of why God allows certain things to happen in our lives, but we should always know that everything happens for a reason. God's thoughts are not our thoughts and his ways are not our ways, but our faith and trust in him helps us to be able to get through whatever the situation might be.

Every day is a new day, one that we have never seen before and one that we will never see again. On this life's side of time, there is no pause button to press to put life on hold and no rewind button to go back to change things that have already happened. So while our eyes have been opened from sleep and we are in our right frame of mind, we need to try to take advantage of every day that God has given us. In this life, time is a constant that has no respect of person. It does not matter who we are, rich or poor, young or old, any nationality; time continues to an inevitable end for each of us. Each night when we close our eyes in slumber, that day is a day that will fade away and become part of our past. As long as God allows us to live and age, time will take its toll on our bodies and our minds. Each day, will be one day further from our sunrise and one day closer to our sunset. We all have an appointed number of days that we will live on this earth. Even though none of us knows when that time will be, we should live each day as if it were our last; because it very well may be.

My hope for each reader of this book is that we would look within ourselves and reflect on events, circumstances and occurrences that we have lived through; then acknowledge and realize the benefits or blessings of each outcome. There can usually be some type of positive silver lining found in every situation, if we look at it with a positive perspective. God is good and allows everything in our lives to happen for a reason. He promised that he won't put more on us than we can bear. May we always try to do unto others as we would have them do unto us.

Marilyn D. Donahue

Contents

Grace for Me

*Unto thee, O Lord, do I lift
up my soul.*

Psalm 25:1 KJV

If I Were Not Here

If this flesh had not been born,
I would not be here to live,
I would not have a chance to serve
Or to have a chance to give,

And touch a soul who asked me
To help her in time of need,
Or give a word of comfort,
Or to plant a calming seed;

If my life had not been given,
I would not be here to share
The words that God inspired
Or the thoughts that came through prayer;

I would not be here to witness
Everything that God has made,
Every blessing he has given
Or the foundation that he laid;

To offer me Salvation
Then for me to understand,
That I didn't have to be here,
Though it was all part of his plan;

God knew before I was born
What my life was meant to be,
He guided and ordered my steps
And allowed my heart to see;

That without him, I am nothing,
Without his love, without his grace,
I would be lost forever,
But he died and took my place.

So, I'm thankful God allowed me
To be on this life's side of time,
To acknowledge and to praise him
With a spiritual frame of mind;

There's one thing I know for sure,
One thing that is very clear;
God has a purpose for me,
If he didn't, I would not be here.

Pray without ceasing.

I Thessalonians 5:17 KJV

A Morning Prayer

My spirit was uneasy,
So I went to sit outside,
To have a little talk with God,
In whom I knew I could confide;

The morning sun was rising,
As I expected it would do,
The clouds were dissipating
As the rays came shining through;

The morning sun was rising,
I looked above in reverent awe,
The beauty of God's glory
Was revealed in what I saw;

The dawn was coming quickly,
As I stared into the sky,
I thought about God's goodness
As the clouds were passing by;

And in that quiet moment,
While reflecting on God's Word,
My thoughts were interrupted
By something I thought I heard;

A faint sound like a small voice,
Like a whisper in my ear;
That he would be there with me,
That I'd have nothing to fear;

If I through faith, would trust him,
Then be patient and be still,
He'd fight my battles for me,
As according to his will.

My mind paused for a second
And I had to say a prayer,
To thank God for his mercy
And to thank him for his care;

My spirit felt much lighter,
As the sun came into view,
And just as I had trusted,
I knew he would help me through;

So, no matter what I'm feeling,
Or what's allowed to come my way;
I know that God will help me
And he'll hear me when I pray.

*The Lord is my light and my salvation; whom
shall I fear? the Lord is the strength of my life;
of whom shall I be afraid?*

Psalm 27:1 KJV

Unknown Presence

Wrong decisions had me going
To a place I did not know,
I searched to find a path out,
But couldn't see which way to go;

I thought that I was trapped there
With no way for me to leave,
But then my heart sensed something
That I barely could perceive;

A presence that was near me
Though I could not see it there,
I felt its calm existence
Totally engulf the air;

I moved and it moved with me,
As if there to watch and guide,
To be there as protection
And remain there by my side.

I was not scared or frightened,
My unease melted away;
I didn't know what this thing was,
But I wanted it to stay;

It beckoned me move forward,
So I followed where it led
And soon my path was made clear,
I could see the way ahead;

Next time when I'm discouraged
And I don't know what to do,
I'll be still and remember
The calm presence that brought me through.

Search me, O God, and know my heart:
try me, and know my thoughts:

Psalm 139:23 KJV

Perceptions

Webster defines perception
As understanding of the mind,
Discernment, intuition,
Apprehension of a sign;

An act of full awareness
Or a knowledge or insight,
Instinctive comprehension
That helps contrast wrong from right.

Perceptions are created
By events within our past,
Experiences we've gone through,
Thoughts and feelings that may last;

A thought you may have lived with
While growing up as a child,
Traditions learned from family,
Some thought strict, then others mild;

A word that is remembered
Or a smell that fills the air,
A song heard from long ago
That transports your mind elsewhere.

Thoughts mold how we view the world,
Each occurrence we perceive,
Those we dismiss as untrue,
Then those we maintain and believe;

To live our physical existence,
Everything we know and feel,
What we think about ourselves
That within our hearts reveal;

The substance of our being,
Born of flesh as mortal man,
To then struggle with the Spirit,
Though we cannot understand;

Why God allowed us free will,
To make decisions on our own,
Those choices are determined
By perceptions we have sown.

Proverbs chapter three, verse five,
Says to trust in the Lord,
Not to lean on understanding
That's based on our own accord,

Or on things that are not just
Or on things that are not true;
God gave us a mind to think
To do what we know right to do.

Whatsoever things are lovely
Or of virtue to perceive,
I pray to think on these things
And within my heart believe;

That one day my thoughts won't matter,
'Cause man's days on earth are few,
My soul will become immortal
And my perceptions will be made new.

Humble yourselves in the sight of the Lord, and he shall lift you up.

James 4:10 KJV

Deep Within

I had a certain feeling
That I just could not describe,
I don't know where it came from,
But it settled deep inside.

I tried and tried to shake it,
But it would not go away,
It stayed with me a long time,
Then I had to kneel and pray;

Oh Lord, what is this feeling
That you allowed to come to me?
Something that I need to know
Or something I need to see?

I know it has a purpose,
Though I do not understand,
Please give me strength to endure
Those things I know are in your hands;

So whatever is your reason
This is meant for me to feel,
I know it's not an accident,
It is according to your will.

Wherever I am led to go
Or whatever I need to do,
I pray Lord you be with me,
That your grace will help me through;

Then Lord, if you reveal it
And so make my mind aware;
From deep within I'd be thankful
For an answer to my prayer.

*Preserve me, O God: for in thee do
I put my trust.*

Psalm 16:1 KJV

Trusting Your Word

I don't know what's before me,
I take one day at a time,
My moments are not promised,
So I leave the past behind;

I only have the present
That controls my life right now,
God's gift of breath each second
That I unwrap, but don't know how;

The time that he allows me
And the grace that he has shown,
Is beyond my understanding
Or anything I've ever known;

Lord, I know you won't put on me
Any more than I can bear,
So whatever I may go through,
I will handle it through prayer;

You know me because you made me
And you know my heart within,
You know that I am trying
To live a life that's free of sin;

Whatever you may have for me
And wherever I may go,
I know it's for a reason,
'Cause you said it must be so;

And as long as I am living
On this earthly side of time,
I'll trust my life to your Word
And continue in my climb;

To one day get to Heaven,
Where I know I want to be,
Where my troubles will be over,
And my soul will be set free.

And the fruit of righteousness is sown in peace of them that make peace.

James 3:18 KJV

Character

Webster defines character
As the features we hold within,
Qualities of behavior
And attributes that we defend;

Developed from our childhood
Are those traits that help define,
The person that we have become
Or the person we left behind.

God knows we are not perfect,
He left his Word as our guide,
To show us how we could live
If we study and abide;

And keep those traits within us,
Like integrity and love,
Honesty and uprightness,
Traits that come from up above;

Then with a spiritual perspective,
All things will have a different view;
Those old thoughts will be pushed away
And that old man becomes new.

Our character should be Holy,
Pleasing to God in all our ways;
That he may bless our efforts
And reward our faithful praise.

Have mercy upon me, O Lord; for I am weak:
O Lord, heal me; for my bones are vexed.

Psalm 6:2 KJV

Body and Soul

This body has a lot of scars,
It has many aches and pains;
It's had some bumps and bruises
And it suffers stress and strains;

It's been through falls and accidents,
Through burns and surgeries;
Some things are long forgotten,
Others left clear memories,

But there's one thing I know for sure,
That no matter the frame it holds,
No matter what this body goes through,
It is protection for my soul.

My soul that is eternal,
My soul, the thing that makes me, me,
My heart, my mind, my spirit,
Everything I'm meant to be;

My soul, that is my conscience,
Everything that I perceive,
My thoughts, my trusts, convictions,
Everything that I believe;

My soul, that God had given,
Even before time had begun,
He knew me in his Omniscience,
He knew the race I'd have to run.

Lord, you know how you made me
And you know my heart within,
You know where I am headed
Because you know where I have been;

Every day that my eyes are opened
And for as long as I am here,
I'll be thankful for this housing
And the treasure it holds so dear.

Father, thank you for your mercy,
And for this body that you gave,
But more so for my spirit;
That you washed and cleansed and saved.

*But God commendeth his love toward us,
in that, while we were yet sinners,
Christ died for us.*

Romans 5:8 KJV

God Loved Me Anyway

Despite my imperfections,
Despite some things that I had done,
Despite the path I followed
Without listening to anyone;

Despite my lack of saying
Things I knew that I should say,
God still had mercy on me
And he loved me anyway.

He reached down to earth from heaven
And he touched my weary heart,
He touched my soul and washed me,
Then gave me a brand new start;

Me, as a mortal being,
Me, whose life was mired in sin;
Me, who had no knowledge
Of the strength I held within;

I had no way of knowing
That God would save one such as me,
Then mold and shape my old life
Into what he knew I'd be;

A sinful soul that's trying
To live a Christian life each day,
And even when I would fall,
I could get back up and pray;

'Cause God said he wouldn't leave me,
That he'd stay right by my side,
If I kept my faith in his Word,
He would in my heart abide;

And help me learn the lessons
From those things that I had done,
That I may continue striving
In this race I have to run.

I never will be perfect,
God didn't say I had to be,
But he knows my heart is willing
To walk the path he set for me;

So, I'm thankful for forgiveness
And his blessings every day;
To show me grace and patience
And to love me anyway.

The Lord looked down from heaven upon the children of men, to see if there were any that did understand, and seek God.

Psalm 14:2 KJV

God Reached Down

Before I became a Christian,
I didn't truly understand
That God already knew me
And he knew my life firsthand;

Because of his Omniscience,
God already knew my heart,
He knew I was not perfect,
But he offered me a new start;

He knew that I would need him
In the pardon of my sins,
He knew that I would trust him
To change the person I had been;

Then God reached down from heaven
To save a sinner such as me,
To wash and cleanse my old life,
Into what he knew I'd be;

A Christian in his image,
Striving each and every day,
To give him praise and glory
In everything I do and say.

I know it won't be easy,
God didn't say that it would be,
But I trust in the scripture
And what those words spoke unto me;

That I must obey commandments
And live according to God's will,
Endure the trials of this life,
Until all things are revealed;

My Spiritual eyes were opened
And I truly understood,
That my work is not meant for me,
But for someone else's good;

We're here to help each other
When we see someone in need,
Then share what God has given
And pray to plant a spiritual seed;

So as long as I am living,
I know my life is not my own;
God saved me to help others
And I will never be alone;

Because we each have a purpose,
God reached down to touch each soul;
That we may be used by his hand,
To help others be made whole.

The steps of a good man are ordered by the Lord:
and he delighteth in his way.

Psalm 37:23 KJV

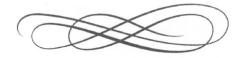

Ordered Steps

Even before my first breath
God knew what my life would be,
He knew that I would be here,
He had angels watching me;

To guide me through those moments
When I didn't understand
And even when I made mistakes,
God held me in his hand.

I learned life has an order,
You can't sing before you talk,
You can't read before you learn how,
Nor can you run before you walk;

If certain things don't happen,
Other things can't come to be,
Everything has its own time,
Even those we cannot see.

Had I not suffered through trials,
Some that happened long ago,
I would not have learned the lessons
That would mold and help me grow;

To trust the Holy Scripture
When I'm weary in my soul,
When I'm feeling down and broken
And I need to be made whole;

Because I'm here for a reason,
God has a purpose just for me,
Something I may need to do
Or something I need to see;

I don't know what it might be,
But I know God is aware
Of everything before me
'Cause he knows what I can bear;

I'm thankful God ordered my steps
Beyond the place that I had been,
He knew my mind was ready,
'Cause he knew my heart within;

To change my way of thinking
To the person I've become,
Who had to learn to trust God
In this race I've had to run.

God's thoughts are not my thoughts
And his ways are not my ways,
So, I pray he orders my steps
Until the end of all my days.

I will call upon the Lord, who is worthy to be praised:
so shall I be saved from mine enemies.

Psalm 18:3 KJV

Hindsight

Hindsight is the fact or knowledge
Of something after it's occurred,
It is seeing what was not known
Or what was spoken and not heard;

"Hindsight is twenty – twenty",
So says the old storied cliché,
That means a truth acknowledged
When things turn out a different way;

As humans, we have our own thoughts
Of how we may want things to be,
We could have the best intentions,
But other minds may disagree;

There may be times when things happen
And the decisions that we make,
May be thought best at the moment,
But then they turn into heart ache;

Not one of us is perfect,
But God has blessed us with a mind
To learn from our experiences
When the truth is hard to find;

We can't see into a man's heart,
Only God knows what is there:
Our motives and intentions,
Every thought and every care;

Every reason and perception,
Every belief that's understood
According to our discernment,
Whether meant for ill or good;

So, there is no way we can lean
On the understanding of man,
God already knows our hindsight
Because our life is in his hand;

It is not for us to question
Why God allows some things to be,
We have to trust that he knows
Everything that we can't see,

Then when he reveals our hindsight,
We can see those things anew,
And know that God was with us
In everything that we went through.

I will praise thee, O Lord, with my whole heart:
I will shew forth all thy marvellous works.

Psalm 9:1 KJV

My Road Map

Within my realm of thinking
In this world of mortal man,
There is so much I don't know,
So much I do not understand;

This physical world around me
Rules my life's realities,
Each day is structured by time,
My decisions, wants and needs.

For now, I'm bound by this world,
It is the only life I know;
Though I'm in it, I'm not of it,
There's somewhere else for me to go;

God left my soul a guide book,
The road map to my new life
And the example I should follow,
To get beyond my fears and strife;

Beyond the cruel injustices,
Earthly heartaches, tears and pains;
Beyond my physical ailments,
Beyond life's stresses and its strains;

My road map is the Bible,
For me to study and believe;
Christ's life is my example,
His words of comfort to receive;

Christ's example is to be Holy,
No matter what I may go through;
To be good and kind to others
In everything I say and do;

Even when I've been mistreated
And misused by my own friends,
I say a prayer for them and trust
That God sees my heart within;

And as I read my guide book,
It will help me to endure
The trials suffered in this life
And the one thing I know for sure;

That one day when God is ready
And my time on earth will end,
My road map will be folded
And my new life will begin.

But he giveth more grace, Wherefore he saith,
God resisteth the proud, but giveth grace
unto the humble.

James 4:6 KJV

God's Grace is Sufficient

Sometimes I feel so burdened
With the cares and toils in life,
It seems there's always something
To cause some misery and strife;

Sometimes I get distracted
And let these cares disturb my mind,
Then I search the Word to help me
Leave these worries all behind;

I cannot always understand
What God allows to come my way,
But I know that he is able
To guide my footsteps every day;

God's grace is sufficient
When I have sinned and been wrong,
It covers my human failings
And it allows me to be strong;

To not do those things I used to do,
To help others who cannot see,
To know that they can be saved,
'Cause he saved one such as me.

Even as I don't deserve it,
God has blessed my repentant soul,
He gave me strength and courage,
He cleansed my heart and made me whole;

Everything for a reason,
Everything in its own time,
God has a purpose for me
And in his Word, I must abide;

'Cause God's grace is sufficient
For anything I may go through,
For anything that he plans for me,
For anything that I must do;

I'm thankful for God's mercy
And the grace he chose to give,
For the love that he has shown me,
For the chance that I could live;

Beyond the cares of this world,
Beyond the things my eyes can see,
Beyond this physical body,
And live with him eternally.

*For with the heart man believeth unto
righteousness; and with the mouth confession
is made unto salvation.*

Romans 10:10 KJV

A Change of Heart

We can't know a man's true heart,
Only God can look inside
And judge his thoughts and motives
That his words may try to hide;

But despite our human failings,
God is faithful to forgive,
If we would ask his mercy
And seek a better way to live;

'Cause God can change that old man
From the man once known before,
Into a brand new creature,
That isn't sin filled anymore;

Once that decision is made,
Despite however he has been,
God can forgive past actions
And see the new heart held within;

His inner man is transformed
And sees life through spiritual eyes,
His perspective is now different
And his mind must realize,

That there may still be struggles,
It takes time to put away
Things that need to be denied
And keep those that need to stay;

The old man has not vanished,
But a new man's in control,
New thoughts, new mind and new heart,
A new outlook for his soul;

It just takes a little faith,
The size of a mustard seed,
But that can move a mountain
When all fear and doubt are freed;

God said he would not leave us,
We would not be left alone,
The Holy Spirit guides us
Until we move to our new home.

Eternal Grace

*Let us therefore come boldly unto the throne of grace,
that we may obtain mercy, and find grace to help
in time of need.*

Hebrews 4:16 KJV

Wings of Grace

Grace is unmerited favor,
It's not earned by words or deeds,
God gives it as he chooses,
A Holy blessing to receive;

Grace is pardon, forgiveness,
Divine virtue from above,
It is mercy and compassion,
The longsuffering of God's love;

Which he extends to my soul
In the pardon of my sin,
If I would trust his guidance
From the place where I had been;

God knows I am not perfect,
Yet he made a way for me
To humbly seek his favor,
Despite my frail carnality;

When trouble is around me
And I feel tossed to and fro,
I seek the shadow of God's wings
When I need a place to go;

To shelter from the turmoil,
From the trials and from the storm,
To gain strength when I'm weary
And to keep me safe from harm;

God offers me protection
Under wings of loving care,
Within his arms of comfort
In a refuge sought through prayer;

'Cause I have not the power
To fight battles on my own,
I seek God's strength and courage
From those seeds of faith once sown;

He promised to be with me
And to never leave my side,
If I trust in the scripture
And to let his Word abide;

Within my life and my heart,
Then surrender to his will,
To be used as a vessel
For his purpose to fulfill;

Lord, thank you for your mercy
And allowing me a place
Of shelter and redemption,
Under eternal wings of grace.

The Lord is my shepherd:
I shall not want.

Psalm 23:1 KJV

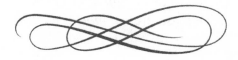

Our Ultimate Example

Webster defines "example"
As part character of the whole,
Something to be imitated,
An illustration to behold;

This thought, we need to keep in mind
When we've seemed to lose our way,
When our lives feel so burdened down
That we have to stop and pray;

'Cause living in this carnal world
Requires decisions every day,
From what we wear or where we go,
To what we do or what we say.

Sometimes this life can seem so hard
When we do not understand
Or see what's around the corner
With these eyes of mortal man,

But we have an example
Of the virtues that we need
To live a life of purpose,
If we study to succeed;

Jesus is that example
Of the way that we should live,
He's our ultimate example
Of the way that we should give;

Christ's example of his goodness,
Is any blessing we might receive,
Even though we don't deserve it
He still provides for all our needs;

Then compassion shows his kindness,
Gentle love given to a soul
Who may be lost, seeking refuge,
In the hopes to be made whole;

Christ shows us of his courage
When he spoke against the tide
Of those who would denounce him,
Without any scorn inside;

As we should speak with boldness,
Despite any trial we may bear,
Our faith gives us that courage
And strength to overcome through prayer;

Yet still, he's an example
Of pure truth and honesty,
No guile was found within him,
He, no other way could be

Hebrews six and eighteen, says
It's impossible for God to lie,
His virtue comes from heaven,
A sinful tongue, we must defy.

God made us in his image
With a mind and with free will,
With a heart and thought of purpose,
With a destiny to fulfill;

Life may not always be easy,
But we have a model and guide,
Our ultimate example
To help us in his Word abide.

We are confident, I say, and willing rather to be absent from the body, and to be present with the Lord.

II Corinthians 5:8 KJV

Just Passing Through

Today, we laid a friend to rest
'Cause God called him by his name;
He touched us with his caring,
We will never be the same;

God said his work was over,
The job he had on earth was done;
His accomplishments in this life
And the race he had to run;

He left his spirit with us,
One of kindness and of love;
Traits that were within him,
That only came from up above;

Even though we will miss him,
Our memories of him will be
A sober, thoughtful reminder
Of our own mortality.

One day, this pain will be eased
And thoughts of him will bring a smile;
The tears may then be lessened,
It might just take a little while.

We know what scripture tells us,
We are only passing through;
That this old world is not our home,
Our home is out beyond the blue;

Where there will be no worries,
No more cares and no more tears,
No physical, mortal body,
No more pains and no more fears.

We do not know our last day,
Only God knows when it will be;
Until then, we're just passing through,
To live with God eternally.

*The earth is the Lord's, and the fulness thereof; the world,
and they that dwell therein.*

Psalm 24:1 KJV

A World Shaken

In this time of reflection,
There is true uncertainty,
Our lives have been disrupted
By a germ we cannot see;

It spreads among the living,
Unbeknownst unto it's host,
It ravages the body,
Damaging what it needs most;

Mortality numbers growing,
It has no respect of man,
Rich or poor or young or old,
We struggle to understand;

This virus that has developed,
Something never seen before,
It's shaken our existence,
Mankind's changed forevermore;

God allowed something so tiny,
Unseen to the human eye,
To make us change our habits
From the fear that we might die;

Despite the pain of this trial,
There is one thing we should see,
That what God allows to happen,
Is how he intends it to be;

He looks down on the whole world,
Everything is in his hand,
We know there is a purpose
Though we may not understand;

But if we believe the scripture
That God left us as a guide,
No matter what we go through,
We should in his Word abide;

And then, wait upon the Lord
To renew our strength each day,
To run and not be weary
In the things that come our way;

'Cause God won't put more on us
Than he knows that we can bear,
Whatever he brings to us,
We can get through it with prayer;

Then when the shaking has ceased
And our hearts are quiet and still,
We'll know that the whole purpose,
Was according to God's own will.

*Now faith is the substance of things hoped for, the
evidence of things not seen.*

Hebrews 11:1 KJV

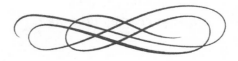

I Can Only Imagine

I've only heard about it
And only read how it will be;
I can only imagine
Just how beautiful to see;

The pearly gates of heaven
And the streets of solid gold,
The beauty of the angels
And the Lord's face to behold;

The majesty of God's glory
And the precious jeweled array,
The sweet angelic voices
Singing praises every day;

My father and grandmother
And those who've gone on before,
A Spiritual reunion
As they greet me at the door;

I can only imagine
Walking to my mansion there
My robe and crown are waiting
In my new home in the air;

A crystal clear, pure river,
Like nothing ever seen before
In it life giving water,
That flows on forevermore;

And then a tree next to it,
That bears fruit, twelve of a kind,
One every month of the year,
Holy meant by God's design;

Then I have to imagine,
No more pain or hate or fears,
No anger, lies or sorrow,
No more death or weeping tears;

Because we know that one day,
This old world will pass away
And I will only imagine,
Living in heaven every day.

*And let us not be weary in well doing: for in due
season we shall reap, if we faint not.*

Galatians 6:9 KJV

Seeking Eternity

This world is filled with heartaches,
With sorrows and tears and pain,
Dishonesty and pressures,
Cruel intentions, ill-gotten gain;

It's not the world, but people,
'Cause this world is ruled by man,
He depends on his own knowledge
In his quest to understand;

The meaning of our purpose,
Of the reason we are here,
He chooses his own pathway,
But that pathway is not clear;

It has pitfalls, diversions,
Things that could entrap your soul,
Deceptions that leave you broken
When you need to be made whole;

But despite how this world may seem,
There's one thing we know is true,
One day this world will pass away
And everything will be brand new;

There will be no more sickness,
No more dying or decay,
No more grief or worry,
All pain will be washed away;

No more fears of injustice,
No more sorrows held within,
No more pleas for mercy,
'Cause there will be no more sin;

This will be Eternity,
Where time will exist no more,
Our old man becomes immortal
Over on the other shore;

On that day we'll transition,
A new body we'll receive,
If we're named in the Book of Life
And on God's Word we believe;

Eternity is waiting,
And we pray to see the day,
When our hope and faith are measured,
According to what scriptures say;

Lord, thank you for your mercy
And the chance for us to be,
Christians saved by your grace,
That we could seek Eternity.

To every thing there is a season, and a time to
every purpose under the heaven:

Ecclesiastes 3:1 KJV

An Appointed Time

Ecclesiastes tells me;
To everything there is a season,
A purpose and a moment,
That is allowed for a reason;

A reason when I'm chastened
And a reason for my tears;
A reason for my trials,
And a reason for my fears;

Even when I don't understand
Why things don't go my way;
I know God is in control
And he hears me when I pray.

God knows how much I can bear,
In those times when I can't see;
Just how I would make it through,
Then, he makes a way for me.

There are times of contemplation
To reflect on thoughts within;
And think on where I am now,
Then remember where I've been.

In all that I have gone through
And in all that I have done,
I had to learn the lesson
That my race would not be won;

Until I turn things over
To the One who saved my soul;
And changed my way of thinking
To trust the One who made me whole.

I know that I'm not promised
The next year or month or day;
I have to use time wisely,
And let God's Word guide my way;

'Cause there is an appointed time
That is only meant for me,
And when God says "It is finished",
Then I'll live eternally;

Beyond the gates of heaven,
Over on the other shore,
Across the river Jordan;
And praise God forevermore.

Yea, though I walk through the valley of the
shadow of death, I will fear no evil: for thou art with
me; thy rod and thy staff they comfort me.

Psalm 23:4 KJV

Leaving My House

My house is sound and sturdy,
But it's in need of some repair,
It's made it through some damage
And is standing with lots of prayer;

Some shingles are all thinning
And the window panes are dim,
The joints are getting creaky
And the outside needs new trim;

Even though it is not perfect,
It has a purpose and a goal,
My house is the protection
For my spirit and my soul;

One day, I'll have to move out,
I don't know when it will be,
But that time is getting closer
With every day God gives to me.

I'll have to leave this old house
Because of aging and decay,
I can't live in it forever,
There's an appointed time and day;

A day that only God knows,
One he set before I was born,
He knew this house would serve me,
Although battered and well worn;

I don't want to leave my house,
It's the only place I've lived,
But God said I must transition
Into the new house he will give;

Then after thinking about it,
I have a different point of view;
If I never leave this old house,
I won't receive my house that's new.

I don't know what it will look like,
That detail matters not to me,
All I know is God prepared it,
He knows how my house will be;

So, from this day and then forward,
I'll try to maintain and achieve
The care of this humble temple,
Until the day I have to leave.

*Boast not thyself of to morrow; for thou knowest
not what a day may bring forth.*

Proverbs 27:1 KJV

Another Day

Thank you Lord for another day
That you allowed my life to see,
A day that I did not deserve
Or could ever hope might be;

Within my hours of slumber,
You watched over my tranquil form,
You kept me safe from danger
And you allowed my soul, no harm.

I felt a gentle nudging,
It was you that touched my eyes
And allowed my lids to open
To the rays of your sunrise;

Another day is given,
Where I'm clothed in my right mind,
It did not have to be so,
But you had mercy and was kind;

Another day to thank you,
'Cause you've been so good to me,
You've blessed me beyond measure
With things I can and cannot see.

You blessed me with my family
And you've blessed me with my health,
You've blessed me with my spirit,
Which exceeds my earthly wealth.

I'm thankful for every moment,
Each day to come and in my past;
I'll try to live each new one,
As if it might be my last;

Because, it very well might be,
There're no promises I've received,
I stand upon the Word of God
And the faith I have believed;

Then time, as days, will be no more,
This old world will pass away,
We'll slip into eternity
And will not need another day.

Let the redeemed of the Lord say so, whom he
hath redeemed from the hand of the enemy;

Psalm 107:2 KJV

I've Been Redeemed

There was much for me to change,
There was much for me to do,
I had to make a decision
To change my life and make it new;

I couldn't do it by myself,
I had not the strength on my own,
I had to seek God's wisdom
And the truth his Word has shown;

My soul was lost and mired in sin
And I could not see the way,
I couldn't see the path Christ paved,
Which offered me a better day;

He offered me salvation,
If I would only heed his Word,
To trust, repent and to believe
In the scripture I had heard.

It is not an easy thing
To live a Christian life each day,
But God will give me strength to stand
When I bend my knees and pray.

His blood was shed on Calvary,
He paid a debt I could not pay,
He covered all my mortal sins
And he washed them all away.

It took a while for me to grow
And get to where I am today,
From the way I thought about life,
To the things I do and say;

It also took a while to learn
That I am not here just for me,
I'm here to help some other soul,
As we seek our eternity;

And then I had to understand,
That I would not be the same,
Now that my soul has been redeemed,
I'd have a new body and new name;

I must not stop my learning,
I must endure until my end;
Then heaven will be my reward
And my new life will begin.

*And God shall wipe away all tears from their eyes;
and there shall be no more death, neither sorrow, nor crying,
neither shall there be any more pain: for the former
things are passed away.*

Revelation 21:4 KJV

One Day, It Will Be My Turn

On that day, when it's my turn,
Everything that I have done,
Will be before the Master,
I'll have nowhere else to run.

It will be too late for "sorry"
Or for what I "should" have done;
I won't have time to finish,
Anything that was begun;

I'll leave the cares of this world,
There'll no longer be a need,
To sleep, to work, to worry,
Or to harvest planted seeds;

When God says "it is over",
And I've breathed my very last;
The only thing that counts then,
Is how I have lived my past;

And if my name is written
In the Lamb's Book of Life;
It then will be determined,
If I find peace or I find strife;

One day, it will be my turn
And I'll leave this shell behind,
I will no longer need it,
I'll have a new heart and new mind;

Where there will be no sickness,
'Cause in heaven there are no fears;
There'll be no pain or sorrow,
Heaven has no place for tears.

On that day, when God calls me,
I pray to see him face to face,
And hear the words of "well done",
Then my soul can take its place;

That one day, when it's my turn,
Only God knows when it will be;
My body will stop living,
But my soul will be set free.

Be not forgetful to entertain strangers: for thereby
some have entertained angels unawares.

Hebrews 13:2 KJV

Angels Before Me

There are angels before me
And they know me by my name,
God has chosen and sent them,
I'm the reason that they came.

My earthly years have taught me
That for all there is a plan,
A plan beyond our knowledge
That is held within God's hands.

There are angels before me
That are here to guide my soul,
They watch and guide my footsteps
So that I may reach my goal;

Of walking into heaven,
Where there will be no more tears;
There will be no more sorrows
And there will be no more fears.

My angels are before me
Though with eyes, I cannot see;
Faith allows me to believe
That they are protecting me;

Faith also allows my heart
To know when things go wrong;
They happen for a reason
And I have to then be strong;

For the harm I did not know,
For the times when I've been spared;
I did not have to be here,
But God showed me that he cared;

He cared enough to touch me,
With his grace and tender love;
Grace that I did not deserve,
Grace that came from up above.

But he that shall endure until the end;
the same shall be saved.

Matthew 24:13 KJV

Not Too Late

These days are filled with troubles,
Trials emerging all around,
Violence, tensions, unrest,
Consolation is not found;

In those who seek destruction,
Without regard to human life,
Their hearts seem filled with hatred,
Conflict, division, fear and strife;

Job chapter fourteen, verse one,
Says man's life is of few days,
He that is born of woman,
Is full of trouble in grievous ways;

Scripture forewarns these moments,
That in the last days there will be,
Earthquakes, famines, pandemics,
The beginnings of what we'll see;

Some nations against nations,
Then false prophets will deceive,
The hearts of those who listen,
Then discard what they believe;

Many will be offended
And cause lawlessness and hate,
Disorder will be rampant,
Leading to a callous fate;

But beyond this dismal warning,
Is the truth of what will come;
The Son of man descending
To be seen by everyone;

The sunlight will be darkened
And the clouds will part the sky,
The stars will fall from heaven
And his coming will be nigh;

This whole earth will pass away,
But the Word of God will stand,
No more time for excuses,
Man's judgment will be at hand;

But, it's not too late to change hearts,
Despite the deeds that have been done,
God seeks our true repentance
When there's nowhere else to run;

As long as we are breathing,
There's a chance to make things right,
We must surrender all to him,
To change darkness into light;

'Cause we will have to answer
For the way that we have been,
For the way we treated others,
For those thoughts held deep within;

No one knows when that will be,
Only God and God alone,
We must use our days wisely,
Before it's our time to go home;

Before our last word spoken,
Before our last thought of mind,
Before we take our last breath
And leave this carnal shell behind;

God will be there waiting
For us to walk through the door,
If we're named in the Book of Life,
We'll live with him forevermore.

The grace of our Lord Jesus Christ be with you all.
Amen.

Revelation 22:21 KJV

CPSIA information can be obtained
at www.ICGtesting.com
Printed in the USA
BVHW071531300720
585046BV00001B/126